A GHOST IN WATERLOO STATION

A Ghost in
Waterloo Station

For Barb,
some offerings from the
Slot tower

Bert
December 1, 2007

BERT ALMON

BRINDLE
& GLASS

© Bert Almon 2007

All rights reserved. The use of any part of this publication reproduced, transmitted in any form or by any means, electronic, mechanical, recording or otherwise, or stored in a retrieval system, without the prior consent of the publisher is an infringement of the copyright law. In the case of photocopying or other reprographic copying of the material, a licence must be obtained from ACCESS the Canadian Reprography Collective before proceeding.

Library and Archives Canada Cataloguing in Publication
Almon, Bert, 1943–

A ghost in Waterloo Station / Bert Almon.

Poems. ISBN 978-1-897142-28-8

I. Title.
PS8551.L58G46 2007   C811'.54   C2007-902551-X

Cover photo: istockphoto.com
Author photo: Geoff McMaster

Alberta Foundation for the Arts

Canada Council for the Arts   Conseil des Arts du Canada

Brindle & Glass is pleased to thank the Canada Council for the Arts and the Alberta Foundation for the Arts for their contributions to our publishing program.

Brindle & Glass is committed to protecting the environment and to the responsible use of natural resources. This book is printed on 100% post-consumer recycled and ancient-forest-friendly paper. For more information, please visit www.oldgrowthfree.com.

Brindle & Glass Publishing
www.brindleandglass.com

1 2 3 4 5 10 09 08 07

PRINTED AND BOUND IN CANADA

For Olga

Contents

I. **The Undertow**
The Muse in the Surgical Theatre — 2
The Undertow — 3
The Only Words of My Bryson Grandmother — 5
Hesitation Before Birth — 7
First Haircut — 9
My Greatest Show on Earth — 10
My Classmate, Janis Joplin — 11
Reading the Road Map — 12
My Alien Encounter — 14
My Brief Career as a Cosmologist — 16
Night Vigil, Evergreen Cemetery — 17
Dead Simple — 18
Stroke Victim — 20
My Ménage à Trois — 21

II. **A Ghost in Waterloo Station**
Hampstead Elegies — 24
10 Kensington Church Walk — 26
Ode to the Hot Water Bottle — 27
Hedgehogs — 28
St. Cuthbert and the Sea Otters — 31
Three Jolly Butchers of Sussex — 32
The Landlord's Dog — 34
Sir Philip Sidney's Shaving Mirror — 35
Dove Cottage — 37
The Immortal Druggist — 38
The Apprentice Pillar, Rosslyn Chapel — 40
A Stop in Heptonstall — 42
A Corona for Grinling Gibbons — 44

The Persistence of Folly — 46
Cargoes — 49
Northern Pastorals — 51
A Ghost in Waterloo Station — 53
Absence of Ultramarine, Presence of Indigo — 55
Kapitalplatz, Salzburg — 56
Overexposure — 58
Olympia — 59
New Guinea Tongue Orchid — 62
Glen Iris Tram — 63

III. Feeding the Power Grid
Moon Towers — 66
Feeding the Power Grid — 68
East Coulee — 69
Armageddon at Endiang, Alberta — 71
Van Horne — 72
Bears — 73
Spanghew — 75
Reconnaisance Flight — 76
Fires — 78
The Cartoonist — 80
The Gargoyle — 81
Dust of History — 82
Value Village — 83
The Shot Tower — 84
Between Heaven and Hell — 85
Wanting as a Tendency to Act — 86
The Seven Deadlies Updated: A Pageant — 88
My Winter Sport — 90

The Holy Family — 92
D'Arcy Wentworth Thompson — 94
Honeysuckle — 96
Tiger's Eye — 98
Austin City Limits — 99
Austin Odyssey — 101
Indian Lodge — 104
Covered with White Cloth, the Grail
Enters the Chapel Perilous — 106
The Feast of St. Valentine's — 107
Frieze of Life — 109
Leonid Shower — 110
Ada Sweet — 112
Coffeewood Court — 114

Acknowledgements — 116
About the author — 118

I. The Undertow

The Muse in the Surgical Theatre

My muse watches with the transplant team
as they wait for the exuberant moment
when the first golden drop of urine
forms at the end of the cut ureter
of the newly-grafted kidney

Then she smiles behind her mask
remembering the day that Pegasus
dug his moon-shaped hoof
into the slope of Mount Helicon
and the first drops of water
formed in the Hippocrene Spring

My muse doesn't flinch or turn away
as she contemplates a drop of urine
so absolutely pure
that it falls without harm
into the body cavity of the patient
Now the surgeon can finish the work
that looked so much like violence

The Undertow

1.
In the days that I waited for my biopsy results,
I sat in the wicker chair in the garden
and watched the purple flowers of the lunaria,
the silver dollar plant. After the flowers come
the green disks of the seed pods. Rub them,
and the pearly circles emerge. Under the living green
find the opalescence, then dry the plant,
put it in a vase on a plain wooden table,
creating a constellation of little moons.

In the garden I imagined a tug at my sleeve,
and I thought of the undertow my parents
always warned me about at the beach.
They never told me that the only hope
is to give in to it, let it carry you out
to some point where you can swim to shore.
It is never the shore you started from.

2.
Floating, drifting, I remembered safe places,
like the grassy lane beside the house
on St. Augustine Street. There was a fig tree,
and a long stretch for my bicycle.
The two chihuahuas, Pancho and Pépe,
seemed the only menace on my journeys.
But once my father was mowing our bit of lane
with his shirt off and ran into a bush,
disturbing a nest of yellow jackets. He screamed,
and it was nothing like the funny scenes
in the funny papers, the Katzenjammer Kids
tormenting the Captain and the Inspector

with hornets' nests: there was always a plunge
into the safety of a pond, and spankings afterward.
As my mother applied the baking-soda compresses
to her moaning husband, she counted nineteen stings.

3.
How many scenes of that lane I remembered
as I floated offshore, looking for the way
to an easy beach. Then it came back, the day
I was chasing Martians with my ray gun.
and ran into a clothesline at neck level:
I stood choking, my eyes wide open
but with a dark lid like smoked glass
closing over them for a moment. I think
the humming sound in my ears
was the clothesline wire, an odd instrument
struck to a single note. I couldn't sing to it
then, but I am doing so now, giving
my fears a voice, giving my voice its fear.

The Only Words of My Bryson Grandmother

Her cloche hat is pulled down to her eyebrows
and the fur collar on her cloth coat
would normally count as trim. But today
there is a rare frost. The boy beside her,
my father, wears knickerbockers
and lace-up boots, and I can count every hook:
the camera gives eternal life to fashion.
The background shows an ornamental plum tree.

The only words of my Bryson grandmother
I've ever read are written on the back of the photo:

Don't I look a sight
but the icycles on plum tree
is very pretty

I would not correct her words
except to say that hoar frost
is so rare where she lived
that few people have the name for it.

I could not correct her words,
knowing she left school at fifteen
to marry a cotton farmer,
knowing she wrote mostly to her mother,
who was in the mental hospital
and therefore reputed to have died long before.
My grandmother would die without pretense,
of angina pectoris—meaning simply pain in the chest—
as my father would in his own time,
at forty-seven, three years short of her span.

I am glad a frosty morning called for a picture.
In an hour or two the sun that made them squint
would melt the frost, send water
dripping from the branches
and down the trunk to the ground.

I would correct everything
but nothing can be corrected.

Hesitation Before Birth

"Hesitation before birth. If there is a transmigration of
souls then I am not yet on the bottom rung.
My life is a hesitation before birth."

— Franz Kafka, *Diaries*

1.
I hesitated. For weeks.
Then I was ready, it seemed,
in the middle of a hurricane,
and my mother made her trip to St. Mary's
in a motor launch. She loved to tell about that.
The marshes around the city bred
crawling and creeping things.
Perhaps my belated soul
was still swimming in the storm-roiled waters,
intimidated by the pincered crayfish,
by the fanged water moccasins
coiled on the lower rungs of the ladder of life.
The alligator's young took refuge in her mouth,
safe in those deadly jaws,
her leathery tail thrashing in the sedge.

My Aunt Minnette was ready for the storm:
she had a garage full of canned food.
The only part of her house to flood was the garage,
and the labels floated off, making dinner
a surprise for months: would it be peaches
with stewed tomatoes? One night
the match was perfect: spam and applesauce.
Hearing this story told and retold,
I learned to be prepared to be unprepared.

2.
My mother came ashore at the hospital
but I was reluctant to make my own landing,
so from her womb I was tardily ripped.
She liked to show me the dark scar when she was angry—
that wasn't fun like hearing about the boat ride.
The Rh factor made the doctors anticipate
a blue baby, but I was a squalling red
and I've declined to be blue ever since.

First Haircut

The first haircut I can remember
was the time I could finally sit
in the deep soft chair: "No,
he won't need the board, Sam,"
my father told the barber. But
Sam cranked the chair high as it would go.
From the side of my face I saw
a mummy-wrapped head in a hot white towel.
Well, no one could shave me yet.
His barber was stropping the razor
with a wick-wick-wick-wicked sound.

Eddie, the black shoeshine boy
with gray in his hair,
made everyone laugh, asking me
if I wanted my Buster Browns shined.
The scissors snipped around my ears,
I remember that, and the Yankees
were on the radio. They must have won,
they always won. Anointed with a hair oil
smelling like coconut from a red bottle,
I was slicked down and ready
for the world of men. Sam pulled off the sheet,
lowered the chair and said,
"That'll be four bits, or is your daddy paying?"

My Greatest Show on Earth

My parents prepared me for my first circus
by telling me about the great Ringling Brothers Fire
of 1944 in Hartford, Connecticut:
it had rained for days and the circus put up a tent
soaked in paraffin. It went up like flame in a flue
and one hundred and sixty nine died, mostly children.
I couldn't understand how the fire had burned
without the rain putting it out.

The day we went was sunny
I sat on the bleachers and kept looking up
at the tent and under the stands
wondering where the flames would start
My father told me to look at the lion tamer
but I knew we had our heads in a lion's mouth
and teetered on a high wire of disaster.
I did look at the line of elephants
and understood why the baby
held so tight to his mother's tail.

The next week at the beauty shop
my mother—a natural blonde—
was having her eyebrows dyed black.
I shuffled through copies of movie magazines
as she complained to Trucie,
her beauty operator and family counselor:
"We took him to the circus
and he kept looking everywhere but the ring.
Have you ever heard of such a child?"
All at once I felt like the smallest clown,
the one who comes tumbling last
out of the collapsing fire truck.

My Classmate, Janis Joplin

But where was she? I must have seen her on the playground or even in the classroom. Perhaps she is one of the nameless faces in my school pictures but no one looks unhappy enough. And how to recognize her, chastely sober and a stone–cold virgin? My cousin Linda, who runs her Kountry Klip N Kurl out of a trailer in Woodville, Texas, remembers tormenting her at the high school reunion. I liked Joplin's music only once, at the best party ever given in Northern Alberta. At the start, the host, Pat, was giving demonstrations of the macho method of drinking tequila, salt on the forearm, lime in one hand, many demonstrations, till someone handed him a joint, and after one toke he had to be carried like a fallen soldier to his room as Janis downstairs howled "have another little piece of my heart." Pat missed his legendary party but not the hangover, and there he differed from Janis who had the party and couldn't get up again.

Reading the Road Map

I went out to see the comet,
a little fuzzed ball of light,
but it was Venus that moved me,
brighter than I'd ever seen her
since an early morning in the 50s,
my family lost on a highway
in the middle of the state
on a trip from a new home
to visit the old home.

My parents in the front seat
struggled with the rattling accordion
of the road map, my father swearing
and my mother asking him not to swear.
We were stopped in the middle of an oil field—
drilling towers with lights all around.

I saw Venus through the windshield
and asked my father if we could steer by that,
but he kept trying to read the map
in the faint moon of the dome lamp.
The map had the roads in red and black
like a circulatory system
in my biology textbook.

We were failing to circulate.

Finally my father tried his lighter,
adding a sun to the cold moon
of the dome lamp.

After all these years I've found us:
our precise position as a family
was to be lost in the middle of the state
between one home and another,
with my father cursing
and my mother telling him not to swear,
as he burned a hole in the road map.

My Alien Encounter

Roswell

"give me the ocular proof."
                    — Othello

My mother's friend Geneva
knew I was mad about rocketry,
so she brought me her books on UFOs.
I was polite, but the pictures
were more out-of-focus
than out-of-this world. I wavered
between seeing them
as lampshades or women's hats.
Another looked like my sister's musical top.
Geneva was an early convert to a religion
that began in 1947. She and her husband
would take vacations to Roswell to look for UFOs,
and they always saw them.

The best book she lent me
said that reincarnation comes
through saucer rides to other planets:
the whole solar system is graded
like hotels. Hell is Mercury,
a cinder sizzling in the sun.
I wanted to visit Saturn, stay in a room
with a skylight opening on the rings.

Her mind moved like a weather balloon
caught in the jet stream,
and the next fad was the bog people
of Jutland, pictures of dark leathery beings

preserved by water, and the chemicals
infused from the sphagnum moss.

South of Roswell

The region is full of terrestrial wonders,
like Gila Monsters in black and pink stripes.
Jim White discovered Carlsbad Caverns,
when he saw black smoke
boiling from a vast vent in the hillside.
It was a flight of bats, a million of them,
as if the earth's core were a magician's fire
sending up billows of flying mammals.
But inside, the cave was an eternal 13.3 Celsius.

Outside the park gates, at White's City,
the bus stop was on the boardwalk,
by The Million Dollar Museum
with its 50,000 collectibles in 50 collections.
A loudspeaker invited me over and over
to "See the 6,000 year old Indian mummy!"
The withered face had the color and texture
of a prune. Preserved by dryness,
but he looked like a bog creature.
I stared at him, my first alien,
but he was more indigenous
than any of the gawkers: the real American,
lost among strangers,
he had no ticket home.

My Brief Career as a Cosmologist

The cardiograph machine hummed a little,
spilling out a coil of tape with an inked line
that only my father's doctor could interpret,
like a coded slip from a fortune cookie, meters long.
I spent my days reading science books, right through
my meals in the cafe across from the hospital.
George Gamow explained our existence
in space-time with the world-line, which he compared
to a rubber bar shaped in cross section
like a man. Thin when the man was a baby,
it grew thicker, wriggled as he moved in space,
"attaining a constant shape at the moment of death
(because the dead do not move)," then disintegrating.
"World–threads," Einstein called the world-lines.
His concept of curved space
could fit more than one universe, like the finite one
with a positive curve, making a sphere,
or an infinite one with a negative curve, a saddle shape
very hard to imagine. Gamow diagrammed the models
 as best he could in a white space of his page,
but what was the space around the diagrams?
I could imagine other shapes for the universe:
cylinders, barbells, or forms like the balloons knotted
into animals at the fair, but the terror was to imagine
any of them, finite or infinite, without my father in it.

Night Vigil, Evergreen Cemetery

After his six year old son died of kidney failure,
Alfredo told us that he could only find peace some nights
by going to the cemetery and sleeping on the child's grave.

He was acting out his own *Día de los Muertos,*
when altars are put up for the *angelitos'* visit.
Not that he built an altar to heap with orange marigolds—
the Aztec "Flower of Four Hundred Lives,"
whose bitter scent guides a child's soul on its journey—
not that he brought *pan de muerto*
and skull-shaped candies for its refreshment.

He just lay there in the desert night
where no watchman was needed,
and if the ground shook, it was only
when a freight train approached the cemetery,
running along the fence, then pulling away.

Dead Simple

"If a modern poet maintains that for each individual there
exists an image which engulfs the world, how often does
that image not arise out of an old toy chest?"
                                          — Walter Benjamin

My favorite toy
was dead simple:
slatted balsa wood
to represent a Sabre jet.
Stencils outlined in blue
the pilot's head in his canopy
and the emblems on tail and wings.
Powered by my arm,
it would go nose-down in the grass,
indestructible.

My teacher, Miss Perryman,
married the pilot of a real Sabre F86D
and the whole town followed
his Korean tour in the papers.
There was a photograph of him
standing by the swept-back wing,
with the twenty-four Mighty Mouse rockets
spread out in a fan on the runway
anchored by two Sidewinder missiles.
His war record was one damaged MiG.

After the engine failure,
the line for the prayer service
stretched for two blocks,

so my family went window shopping.
In the jewelry display at Bluestein's
a Timex Waterproof Watch
kept perfect time in its goldfish bowl.

Stroke Victim

The words are as elusive as tying his shoes:
the family smiles discreetly when he says
United Mistakes of America, and just now
he asked for Black Horse Cake for his birthday.
The words are still there, he can sense them.
The other day a thermometer slipped
from his weak right hand. He tried to scoop up
the bright droplets of mercury resting
in the grouting of the tiled floor. He could
move them about but not pick them up
as they slid away always, always slid away,
silver globules too small to return an image.

My Ménage à Trois

Our neighbor Al was a Don Quixote of love:
a Knight of the Mournful Countenance
dressed in a shabby suit with the shoe horn
of his profession in his upper pocket.
His wives proved the odd proposition
that a beautiful bottom could evolve
for the purpose of polishing a bar stool.
His proposition was that the homeliest of men
could come home from a bar with company.

Irene, the German wife, hired me
to take care of their lawn but never paid.
Toni, a Dulcinea of the Dangling Earrings,
did the watering herself
which always brought me outside
to tend the roses along our carport
One summer I watered them till they died.
Proximate Cause of Death: a black halter top.

Al and Toni thought it was unhealthy
that I spent so much time reading,
so they took me on odd dates
to the bowling alley, or to wrestling matches
where Toni would whistle at her favorites
and jump up and down calling for bloodshed.
Afterward they would buy me cokes
and ask why I didn't have a girlfriend.
I was their pimply Sancho Panza.

Toni started a dress shop in Kern Place
years before El Paso knew the word *boutique*.

She and her partner, Sharon, bought little Renaults,
a blue one for Toni and a pink one for Sharon.
Their matching toy poodles
were dyed the same colors.
One day Toni and the blue Renault were gone.
Al had to go questing in the bars again
and I went back to reading on Saturday nights.

II. A Ghost in Waterloo Station

"Every time you pack or unpack your suitcase,
you learn something about yourself."
— Michael McCarthy

Hampstead Elegies

20 Maresfield Gardens

The contents of the house came from Vienna:
now Berggasse 19 is furnished
only with photographs of objects
you'll find here like the famous couch topped
surprisingly with a colorful blanket,
and the green bucket chair. A house
riddled with atmosphere.
The antiquities on the wide desk
and in the cabinets are funeral objects.
I liked the little Egyptian boat
bearing a mummy case to the land of the dead.
It has three kneeling attendants
whose oars are lost. Prow and stern
are long-necked sea serpents. On the deck,
a tall jar for the entrails of the corpse.
Once there was a chart to the land of the dead,
and set answers for those who challenge the soul.

On one display I saw the x-ray
of a jaw eaten by cancer. I looked again
at the frieze from the Roman sarcophagus,
two mended fragments, the seam visible.
It was not the usual scene of Endymion
sleeping in a field, visited by the Moon.
It showed the crowding shoulders
of the mourning Trojans bearing the outsized
and mangled body of Hector above them.

Wentworth House

"—for axioms in philosophy are not axioms until they are proven on our pulses."

The two houses were made into one
by an actress who owned them long after.
Some of the letters are on display
in glass cases covered with blue brocade.
You can lift the cloth to read the browning ink.
Every reading fades them by a tiny increment
but you can't resist. When you reach
the final words, "Good-bye Fanny! God bless you,"
they're too private, replace the cloth quickly
and leave them in a harmless dark.

Outside is the second plum tree,
planted to replace the original
he sat under writing about the nightingale.
The replanting raises the same question
as the poem, about individual and species.
I'm told the basic problem of philosophy
is the relation of universal and particular,
something he asked of the nightingale,
something he asked by underlining
"Poor Tom" in his copy of *King Lear*
when his brother was dead or dying.

10 Kensington Church Walk

Pound's old house
is now a poster shop
with *Kensington Playboy Agencies* upstairs.
Some of the poems were bold as posters
and he managed to keep two households in Rapallo.

The house has no blue plaque.
The campaign failed,
his political odor in the civic nostrils
being very bad.
The house itself had a smell
the poet complained about,
being a man with a vocation for complaints.

He remade literature from this place
before he fell for Mussolini.
Reading his letters you realize
he wanted to make the poems to run on time,
but he became the mad dispatcher
and whole shipments went off the rails.

Across the street the church
still has the bells Pound hated.
He wrote a letter of complaint so witty
that the vicar posted it in the vestry
but didn't mute the bells,
a portent for a prophet.

As a compromise a blue plaque
could be placed in the belfry
to keep company with the bats.

Ode to the Hot Water Bottle

A strange bladder, flat with a plug in its mouth, something my parents had around but never used, leaving me to think it was some kind of sexual device. Welcome on snowy nights in a Sussex farmhouse called Barn Meadow, where the traditional orange one was wrapped in a homemade cloth cover to prevent burning the skin, keeping its heat for hours when filled from the kettle. Welcome also the blue one I used in a farmhouse called Carrigbawn in County Cork near Drinagh, a bottle with a patented feathery surface so no cover was needed. The orthodox placement is under the feet, but I slept with it chest-high without mistaking it for my absent wife, who is neither flat nor given to turning lukewarm then tepid then cold by morning. She is softer than feathers with no menace of burning the skin. Still the hot water bottle is welcome on a cold night in any farmhouse anywhere after the radiators turn cold. Blessings upon it as it plays out the second law of thermodynamics. Blessings upon it though it reminded me that she was across the ocean sleeping alone under a feather bed in a thermostatically stable room, her amiable warmth wasted in the night.

Hedgehogs

Erinaceus europaeus

1.
Only the English hedgehog
could make me give up
my allegiance to the armadillo,
the State Mascot of Texas:
perhaps there's something creepy
about an animal with hair
growing out of its shell. The hedgehog
has straightforward prickles.
Proportionally, the male
has the longest reproductive tract
of any mammal. If you wonder why,
contemplate the mechanics
of mating with a prickly partner.
The spine is admirably flexible
and hollow prickles
adhere in star-shaped clumps.
The slightest menace
and the animal turns into a spiky ball.
We won't speak of the hairy moon rats
of Asia, the spineless cousins.

2.
After months of trying
to lure hedgehogs into our yard,
we got out of the taxi one night
and Olga almost stepped on one.
After that these pub-crawlers
stopped at our local every night.

3.
Alleged milkers-of-cows,
alleged stealers-of-eggs.

Their feeble teeth can't puncture an egg.
but are sudden death to slugs.
Imagine a huge round brush
trying to milk a cow.
Imagine a cow standing for it.

At Leadenhall Market ,
with its silver gryphons
protruding long red tongues,
hedgehogs used to be sold
to be kept in cellars
to eat household insects.

In my yard a pair of them would shuffle along
to the waiting bowl in the light of the porch.

4.
Certain people are hedgehogs:
I know a woman who is a goddaughter
of Mrs. Tiggy-winkle and a bit pricklier.
After our hedgehogs appeared,
Ian Redfern across the street—
devoted worshipper of his roses—
would sneak across at night
to peer over the wall.
Perhaps the roses attuned him
to prickly things. Ian's round head

looked like nothing so much
as a hedgehog.

5.
"The fox knows many tricks,
the hedgehog knows only one,
a good one," so said Archilochus.

One night in Shoreham-by-Sea
we heard a shrieking sound
and looked out the bedroom window
just as the street lamps went off—
an economy measure or a subsidy for burglars.
The full moon was red
and all we could see was a few shapes
scurrying around on the lawn.

Later the neighbors found the bodies
of our two hedgehogs in their yard.
One good trick, but not good enough.

I wanted to write a cheque
to the local Fox Hunt.

6.
My only hedgehog now
is the boot scraper in the hallway,
a pointed iron face fronting
a mound of brown bristle.

St. Cuthbert and the Sea Otters

Cuthbert was a shepherd boy in Scotland till he saw a great light entering the sky escorted by other lights: the Abbot of Lindisfarne had died. The boy walked to the abbey at Melrose and became a monk. After he went to the Holy Island, he liked to live with the seals and the frolicking sea otters. Once when he was washed away by a wave, he was washed back again in good health the following day: the otters had kept his feet warm by breathing on them, which must have tickled though the chroniclers don't say so. He sheltered the eider ducks, which were hunted for their down, and the Northumbrians still call them cuddy ducks in his honor. When he was elected a bishop, he went into hiding until the king and clergy came and implored him to accept, which he did tearfully. He travelled more after his death than during his lifetime, said the Venerable Bede, for whenever the monks of the Holy Island fled the Vikings, they carried their saint, whose body was uncorrupted, with them. One night the monks carrying Cuthbert saw him in a vision: "Bury me at Dunholme," he said. They didn't know where Dunholme was till they overheard a milkmaid say her lost cow had wandered there. So Cuthbert, still uncorrupted, was buried in a fine silk cloth with curious embroideries, and buried with him was the head of St. Oswald, the warrior saint of Northumbria. The tomb was opened after 500 years by the henchmen of Henry VIII who came to despoil it, but they trembled when they saw the Saint was undecayed. When the tomb was opened again after 500 years more the body had reduced to bones at last but the embroideries could still be traced. They were Arabic and said, "There is no God but Allah." On that day in heaven, the sea otters swimming in the crystal stream by the throne of God leaped and tumbled in mirth and one bright light among the transfigured saints turned scarlet for a moment.

Three Jolly Butchers of Sussex

The Romantic

Pete at Gibson & Coe
greets a customer this way:
"I'm feeling very romantic today, madam—
last night I sat down and reread
all the poems of Shakespeare!
Imagine that, a veteran in his armchair,
reading Shakespeare! And I've read
all the poems of Keats,
and not just the famous ones!"

The Undersecretary for Commonwealth Affairs

In one interrogatory sentence
the butcher at Dewhurst's
annuls the Statute of Westminster,
asking my wife,
"And which of the colonies
are you from, madam?"

She wanted to say,
*the one that saved your ass
in the last war, Mister,*
but saying ass when you mean arse
is such a colonial thing.

Thump. Thump. Thump.

"For in thye shoppe is many a flye loos."
                       —*The Canterbury Tales*

The *High Class Family Butcher*
on High Street makes me think
of the meanings of the word "high."
as I look at his flock of plucked chickens
—all of them suffering from a skin disease
He never has any customers,
but spends his day at the cutting table
happily stalking and swatting flies
with his enormous wooden mallet.

The Landlord's Dog

The Old Vine, Cousley Wood, East Sussex

The sun shines through the blossoming cherry
in the front garden of The Old Vine.
At the table behind me the village philosopher
is talking to three women about Nothing:
"You girls answer every question with nothing:
What are you doing?—Nothing.
What did you mean by that?—Nothing
What do you want for lunch?—Nothing.
That's your whole generation, and you don't know
that it's a different kind of *nothing* in each sentence."
I am doing nothing except drinking my Guinness
and squinting at the cherry tree. Petals come down
in the wind once in a while. If I watch one fall
with my right eye, its path is absolute necessity,
with the left eye, absolute contingency.
If I wait long enough, a petal will fall in my glass,
I have that much confidence in cause and effect.

The landlord's old dog, a boxer named Bim,
limps out of the pub, spots a family walking up
the pavement, and barks at them, just to assert
his canine honor and his own sense of causality.
Then he keeps barking feebly at the empty air.
Bim's sense of space and time is muddled,
mine is unequivocally ambivalent.
I look down and see a pink petal floating in my glass.
All the energies of the universe have put it there.

Sir Philip Sidney's Shaving Mirror

Sidney's effects lay on a table at Penshurst:
his funeral helm, and a fragment
of his shaving mirror. The bright helmet
was crested with a porcupine,
something like a greyhound with tusks,
and a few spikes on its back.
The helm was made for the man,
but not to be worn, just carried
before his coffin in the cortège.
In the engravings of the procession,
the heralds bear the hatchments of knighthood:
spurs, gauntlets, helm, the sword and shield,
the coat of arms. Archaic trappings:
the man was killed by a musket shot.
He lay dying for three weeks, the surgeons
probing his thigh for the bullet.
It kept its secret, and only the dying man
would acknowledge the odor of septicemia.
His will breaks off in mid-sentence,
like the manuscript of his *Arcadia*,
which leaves Prince Pyrocles in disguise
and flinching in combat for the first time:
a cliffhanger unplanned, with no sequel.

The playful young poet who called Stella
an absent presence became
a present absence, a rhetorical twist
he would have loved. The nation mourned.

The simpler relic of his unfinished life
is the darkened shard of shaving mirror.
It held his face every day,

but it returned only my shadow
and my breath left no ghost on its surface.
The silvering has tarnished with age:
time painting death's portrait
as a black field, absence made present.

Dove Cottage

Downstairs Bedroom
Double washstands are a rarity
even in antique stores:
the Victorians cut them in half,
unable to bear the lewdness
of a husband and wife
standing together in night clothes
washing their faces.
This one has a cistern underneath
to collect the water for reuse.
Frugality likes the country proverb:
water carried from the well
is never enough.

Kitchen
Frugality ruled the kitchen
where two meals a day were porridge
and the tea leaves were reused
three or four times
before Charity wrapped them in paper
to give to the poor.

Garden
The poet would compose out loud,
pacing up and down the garden terrace,
making his poems about the simple folk
of the Lake District.
One day he wandered into the village
still composing a poem
and one of the simple folk
said to his wife:
"Old Wudsworth's broke loose again
Better tell his family to come get him."

The Immortal Druggist

A Rainy Sunday in London

". . . he has ever since existed in my mind as the beatific vision of an immortal druggist, sent down to earth on a special mission to myself."

→ Thomas De Quincey

A runaway Public School boy
living rough on Oxford Street,
Thomas met a streetwalker:
Ann, 15, not a golden-hearted cliché
but a scared girl who revived him
when he fainted from hunger,
bringing a glass of spiced port.
They kissed once, just before he went back
to his life as a merchant's heir,
and she vanished into "the mighty labyrinths
of London." He never knew her surname.

Years later, he went into a chemist's
on a rainy Sunday, where the druggist,
dull and stupid as the day,
sold him opium for headaches
and became "the unconscious minister
of celestial pleasures." A bitter drug,
dissolved in a tincture of alcohol.
When he went back again,
shop and druggist had vanished.
On Oxford Street, the shop, Oxford Street.

Dove Cottage, 1819

"Of this at least, I feel assured, that there is no such thing as forgetting possible to the mind."
                                                    — De Quincey

Long after the celestial pleasures turned to hell,
he dreamed it was a bright Easter Sunday in Grasmere.
He stood at his garden gate and saw the Alps,
with the towers of Jerusalem like a stain before them.
A bow's shot away, Ann sat on a rock beneath
Judean palms. "I have found you at last,"
he said, just as vapors rolled between them.

What were the Orient spices in that wine?

The Apprentice Pillar, Rosslyn Chapel

A site for *Da Vinci Code* tourists these days,
but the old legends are more interesting.
The ceiling has the faces of the popular story:
the apprentice with the scar on his temple,
the master, his face defaced by rage and envy.
A cowled woman down the aisle
is supposed to be the apprentice's mother.
From her place she cannot see her son.
There are light touches like the angel in the ceiling
playing the bagpipes, and the fox carrying off the goose
with the housewife chasing them across the wall,
but mostly the chapel is covered with the Fall of Man,
the Dance of Death, the Crucifixion, and the Last Judgment.
Errors have crept into the stony text:
misplaced slabs have put Gluttony
into a frieze of the Seven Acts of Mercy,
while in the Seven Deadly Sins tableau
a man is giving water to the thirsty.

The apprentice pillar has eight dragons at the base,
their necks entwined as they bite their own tails.
Four streamers of foliage without fruit
twist around the pillar to the pediment
which shows Isaac on the altar
and the ram caught in the thicket.
Abraham, the figure of helpless love,
was gouged away by the Puritans.
The story goes that the master mason went to Rome
to study models for the pillar,
but the apprentice dreamt a design

and carved the pier. The returning master
killed him with a mallet. The story
is a fable from our collective dream,
with bound victims and anguished mother.

A Stop in Heptonstall

It means "the place of roses,"
but there were never roses.
The church has a meticulous copy
of *The Last Supper*
and a cemetery with the graves
of three poets. The epitaph
of Asa Benveniste reads,
Fool Enough
To Have Been a Poet.
Plath's stone has deep-cut letters:
Even Amidst Fierce Flames
The Golden Lotus Can Be Planted.
We knew that Assia, the woman Hughes
left Plath for, is buried nearby
with their child: she was less
careful when she turned on the gas.
Olga and I didn't look for a stone.

A town of weavers, built on a slope
out of gritstone from the quarry,
which is a favorite for rock climbers.
The forty-five graded routes
have some odd poetry in their names:

Senility
Thin Red Line
Forked Lightning Crack
Cream
Demerara
A Step in the Light Green

Just outside the cemetery
we saw two squabbling cats,
one black, one orange.

"It's Ted and Sylvia,"
Olga said, remembering that Plath
had red-blonde hair. On a canted street
leading to the car park,
we saw a green parrot
in a big garden cage
singing a syncopated riff
imitated from a blackbird
on the roof across the street.
It sounded like a rhumba,
but a couple with jazz festival
t-shirts said, "It's a jazz parrot."
A song from one mouth
transformed in another.
Our powerful car drove up the slope
to the Tops, where the heather
would keep its scorched black
till the spring, when it would turn
all purple and perfume, better
than lotuses, better than roses.

A Corona for Grinling Gibbons

"There is no instance of a man before Gibbons who gave to wood the loose and airy lightness of flowers."
                                              — Horace Walpole

1.
A window can look into a world as well as out to it.
Grinling Gibbons lived alone in a thatched hut
"to apply himselfe to his profession without interruption,"
said John Evelyn, a good diarist and eaveswatcher.
Evelyn peered through the window one day
to see a man carving a crucifixion scene
with an engraving after Tintoretto as his model.
Evelyn brought Gibbons and his panel to King Charles,
who set him to carving great swags of flowers and shells.

2.
Setting himself to carve great swags of flowers and shells
and birds and fruit, Mr. Gibbons filled country houses
and churches with limewood panels and reredos.
The half-size violin at Petworth has strings so fine
you want to play it pizzicato, and his quill pens
could have been pulled from a wooden goose.
His admirers look for the pea pods in his designs,
the shell split open to reveal a row of spheres,
small perfections formed by the chisel and gouge.

3.
Perfections were formed by the chisel and gouge,
chips and curled shavings fell to the table, profusion
emerging from the thin edge of the blade. That day
when John Evelyn stood under the eaves, he discovered

"such a work, for the curiosity of handling, drawing and studious exactness, as I never in my life had seene before in all my travels": a crucifixion rendered in wood, with "above 100 figures of men." A window can look into a world as well as out to it.

The Persistence of Folly

"If the fool would persist in his folly, he would become wise."
— William Blake

The Arboretum, West Dean, Sussex

The painter Zeuxis painted fruit so well
the birds came and pecked at it.
Edward James, owner of West Dean
and patron of Surrealism,
created beech trees of fiberglass and resin
so real that I couldn't find them in the grove,
a kind of *reductio ad rationem*.
The trees are hard to repair:
real woodpeckers gouge nests in them.

Dali lived in a cottage in these woods
in the 1930s. He designed red sofas
for Mr. James in the undulant form
of Mae West's lips, a florid embouchure.
The folk metaphor of American sailors
paid her a better compliment: they dubbed
their bulky life jackets "the Mae West,"
flesh turned into metaphor.

London, New Burlington Academy, 1936

Señor Dali was a voyeur,
never touched a human being.
His wife Galina arranged tableaux

for him, prostitutes of both sexes
in permutations of feigned coitus,
sterile postures in refutation of desire.

He made his affliction into metaphor,
wandering about in a diving suit
at the opening of the Surrealist Show.
When he started to stagger
like a sub-sea Charlie Chaplin,
the crowd laughed, until someone
realized that the man was suffocating.
No historian has explained
how he fitted his moustachios
into the globular helmet.

Portraits of Edward James

Magritte painted him twice:
one portrait shows Edward's body
at a desk, with the head transformed
into an exploding bulb of light.
A man with an idea.

In the other portrait,
he stands facing a mirror
which reflects his back instead of his front.
On the table, a copy of Poe's
The Narrative of A. Gordon Pym,
in which the hero narrates his own death.

The Sundial, Front Face, West Dean

Not a circle: the numbers are arranged
in a rhomboidal shape.
A sundial has no moving parts
except the shadow. At my feet,
a slab is inscribed with a grid
and a complex graph passing
through the months of the year.
A plaque tells how to compensate
for the equinoctial recession
and Daylight Savings time.
With a calculator and a knowledge
of calculus I could correct the readings
and estimate the Greenwich time,
a *reductio ad absurdum* of the real:
it would be a new time when I finished,
as if we pass through duration in a diving suit.

My watch turns limp on my wrist.

Cargoes

Runswick, North Yorkshire

From the cliffs I could see
machines digging black boulders
into the brown-yellow beach:
stones from Norway to shore up the shore.
In the chroniclers' tales, King Canute
tried to turn the tide of the same sea
by fiat but lacked the heavy machinery.
Tell Rupert Brooke there's some corner
of an English beach that's forever Norway.

Sheepscombe, Gloucestershire

We stood with John Workman
looking out over the deep valley
to Painswick, a village replicating his own
John's cottage is No. 1, Far End
He pointed to a high-flying plane,
"That would be going to Kosovo."
We couldn't distinguish
relief planes from bombers at that height
and were left wondering
what Far End means anymore.
We would go to dinner that night
at the celebrated Butcher's Arms.

The next day John served Japanese wineberries
that he grows in his woods:
little fruits like spherical raspberries.

but harder to pick and hard to clean.
They're sweeter and more poignant.

Later I asked my wife
if we could buy the seeds anywhere.
With the pleasure of the Nestorian monks
showing Justinian the silkworm eggs
they'd smuggled out of China in a staff
she displayed the five seeds
she'd picked from her teeth
and wrapped in a tissue.

Northern Pastorals

1.
At Birdoswald the cheviot sheep
had clustered around a gap in Hadrian's Wall.
One of them scratched her head on the stones.
I could imagine how Thomas Hardy
with his double-sided straight-edge
of historical irony
would have described the innocent ewe,
putting the animal alongside
the shades of the Roman garrison.
A good Latinist, he would have recalled
that the root meaning of "innocent" is "unknowing"

Oblivious sheep and ghostly soldiers.

2.
"Leade": a hamlet, named from the Anglo-Saxon *bleodu*, "wood with a shelter."

Down in Yorkshire
on a day of record heat,
we parked by the Crooked Billet Pub.
The only wood in these parts
is the twisted log on its sign
showing how the twig was bent.
The village of Leade has vanished.
It was worth 30 shillings in the Domesday Book.

We entered a sunny field
holding a church too small for its setting.
We passed sheep and a girl
riding a one-eyed horse.

> ST. MARY LEAD.
> This Church is maintained by the
> Redundant Churches Fund,
> St. Andrew-by-the-Wardrobe,
> Queen Victoria St., London.

The tiny sanctuary
had three pulpits
arranged in stair steps.
A redundancy of sermons, I thought.
The unpainted wood has turned as grey
as the stone of the building.
There was barely room in the floor
for the De Tyas and Skargill tombs
with their footworn armorial markings.

Outside again, we saw a flock
of cheviot and black-faced sheep
lying in the shade of the church
ruminating on their morning experience.
Nothing is redundant
if it blocks the afternoon sun.

The girl—
the girl on the one-eyed horse—
had vanished

A Ghost in Waterloo Station

"Death is not an event in life: we do not live to experience death."
— Ludwig Wittgenstein

I lived my minute of death,
not as a body, not even as a skeleton:
in the toilet at Waterloo Station
I looked up from my hands
wringing themselves together under the tap
and saw the basin and the wall behind me
in the mirror, but I wasn't there:
there was no one at all,
my removal more unnatural than dying.
I had never imagined a world
from which I was purely absent.
Had I met the *kannerezed noz*
on a night road without recognizing them,
the ghostly Breton women
who wash the shrouds of the death-fated?

I tilted my head, turned it, trying
to bring myself back by moving
in the mirror, shaking the image into focus.
But there was no image, so finally
I reached out toward my missing body,
and the hand passed through the mirror,
which was not a mirror but empty space.
The two halves of the room replicated
themselves: the walls, the rows of basins
back to back, each a double of the other.
I went through the baffled entrance/exit
into the luminosity of the station

like a confused spirit in the void, moving
against a crowd heading to or from
a platform, and no one's eyes met mine,
till I found the only face in London
that I knew. With her recognition
I could feel the blood pounding in my ears,
and the leather in my shoes which pressed
against the hard floor of the station.

Absence of Ultramarine, Presence of Indigo

Christ in the House of Mary and Martha, National Gallery of Scotland

This is Vermeer's earliest surviving painting,
on the basis of the pigments in the dark blue
of Christ's mantle, which catches our attention
more than the faint nimbus around the head.
The attribution has been challenged, the subject
being religious, therefore not Vermeer.
Christ's parables found the sacred in the ordinary,
but here is the ordinary in the sacred.
The man seated at the table extends
his hand in a friendly gesture. Mary sits
at his feet, chin in hand, while Martha leans
over the table with a basket of bread, oddly more
attentive than her sister, who became the type
of the contemplative. If Jesus says, *Martha, Martha,
thou art troubled and careful about many things*,
he says it as a friend to a friend, not in red type.
In Vermeer's Bible everything is in red or nothing.

Kapitalplatz, Salzburg

I must have gone through the looking glass:

I sit on a park bench and watch two men playing chess
with pieces as high as their knees.
A big grid is marked off in a corner of the plaza
and the pieces look like machine parts
—bolts and cylinders—
except for the two with horse-head silhouettes

Amazing how quickly the men play
hauling the rooks and bishops about
by the handles.
Mozart was a pawn for his archbishop
who could seldom remember his name.
Now there are a half dozen Mozart scholars
who know the bishop's name,
Hieronymus Count of Something-or-Other.

All the famous candies of Salzburg
have marzipan at the center
a sickly-sweet surprise under the bitter chocolate.
The best-known ones are *Mozartkugeln*,
"Mozart Balls." Odd fame in his native city,
where the little yellow trucks at the airport
have his name painted on the sides.

In another hour the carillon will play
a melody from *The Magic Flute*,
but I don't think I'll wait for that.

This must be through the looking glass:
the fountain in the plaza is topped by a Neptune

looking lost so far from the sea.
His stallions that rim the basin
spouting water from their mouths and nostrils
and they have webbed hooves.
I don't consider a winged horse absurd,
but balk at webbed hooves.
Yet there must be a poetry of the ocean floor
burning with salt instead of heavenly fire.

I watch like a condescending prelate from my bench
as the white player lugs a horse's head
in its L-shaped move—
the unaccountable leap of genius—
and the game is over.

Overexposure

"Light has always been considered painless in Greece. How strange!"
 — Odysseus Elytis

A restaurant sign on our way out of Athens
had an octopus with the head of Yosemite Sam.
Two of the tentacles held lemon halves
and it was squeezing juice on itself,
not a classical image, but indelible.
We had lunch at a cafe where the tarred parking lot,
softened in the sun, was scattered with dead moths.
Their grey wings had false eyes, black dots in white circles.
A boy who spoke no English brought a menu
which had no words, just pictures of food
and prices in drachmas with multiple zeros.
I understood the pictographs when I saw
the disco floor beyond the dining room. Empty.
Noon was too early for a tourist bacchanal.

We walked into the sun, which dripped like juice
on my head, my arms. A country where clarity
is inescapable until it forces your lids shut.
The grey moths were still there,
unblinking eyes on their wings.

Olympia

Archaic Body of Hermes

In the museum Hermes stands,
holding the infant Dionysus
in the crook of his left elbow.
The baby stretches toward
something he can see and we can't:
an absent cluster of grapes
held in the missing forearm of Hermes.
The arm with the infant rests
on a tree stump, over which
the god draped his mantle. When the man
who dug up the statue sent a photograph
back to Germany, his colleagues
criticized him for leaving a rag
hanging on the sculpture. Crafty Praxiteles,
creating a *trompe l'oeil* for the future,
mediated by the unimaginable camera.

Wine implicit in the grapes,
a god of wine implicit in the baby,
a vision implicit in the viewer:
the marble poise of movements
and counter-movements in every muscle
of the figures adds up to a zero sum
of motion that you feel
in your own clenched muscles
as you stop yourself from reaching too.

Change your life? You already have.

Gift Shop at a Crossroads

This was the gift: the Frenchwoman
who sold us a disk by Theodorakis,
had the rarest of human eyes, a pure grey.
Theophanies never show up
on my credit card statement.

Pheidio Eimi

All through the Games site
the Judas trees, strictly unbelievers,
bloomed their clusters of mauve flowers.
We looked for the workshop of Phidias,
its floor plan covered with the ruins of a church,
the top layer of the palimpsest, half-erased by time.
The archaeologists doubted this was the workshop,
until a tiny bottle was dug up in shards:
I belong to Phidias was scratched on the bottom,
his only surviving signature, on a cheap jug.

Accused of stealing gold supplied to drape
the ivory Athena he carved for the Parthenon,
he proved his innocence by weighing the draperies,
true measure to the ounce. Then he was charged
with carving himself on the shield of the goddess,
as a bald old man hefting a rock in battle.
As for that, no sculptor throws stones:
he cuts them down to size.

The church built over his workshop
had three aisles, to proclaim the Trinity.
Outside its vanished walls,
the innocent Judas trees seething with flowers
proclaim and fulfill the oracles of spring.

New Guinea Tongue Orchid

Melbourne Royal Botanic Garden

I know about the yucca and the yucca moth,
a strange nuptial pair: the white moth sleeps by day
in the bridal chamber of a yucca flower,
then flies with a ball of sticky pollen
in the pearly moonlight to the pearly blooms
of another yucca. Plant and moth
would be extinct without each other.

The tongue orchid has bloomed
in the glasshouse after thirty years.
The cluster of coral blossoms look like bridal bouquet,
with the ribbon of a long pink leaf hanging from it.
The plant has the orchid's habit of tricking insects,
this one smelling like rotting meat and manure
to attract the blind beetles to pollinate it.
It has dabbed itself with its own *Nuit d'Amour,*
but there are no beetles here, so the jilted bride
waits among bewildered guests holding their noses.

Glen Iris Tram

Route 6, Melbourne

The antique store on St. Kilda Road
is called "Our Elysian Fields"

The eye has a hundred thousand points for focus
but today I select the Elysian field of vision

The tram makes me a moving point of view
my own blue-green iris an opal gathering lights

I can taste paradise along High Street
where orange and lemon trees bear in mid-winter

The manager of the bedding shop at closing time
is fluffing every fat cushion in his window

A man carrying a little palm tree in its pot
has the air of a king with a scepter

The tram passes a gate signposted
INWARD GOODS ENTRANCE

I think I'm stocking up

for Kurt and Deborah

III. Feeding the Power Grid

Moon Towers

"That which depended on nature for light at 7:45 o'clock was at 8 o'clock bathing in the wonders of the Nineteenth Century. In every nook and corner the brilliant lights sent their shooting rays and the whole face of creation was transcendent."
        Austin, Texas newspaper, May 4, 1895

I thought there was a baseball game every night:
I'd look out from the windows of my room
and see the bright lights over toward Nueces Street.

Then one night I was walking back late
from a movie and came across it,
the 175-foot iron tower
with a cluster of six mercury vapor lamps.
Not bright enough to be a good street light.

I asked around and was told: one of the moon towers.
Built in 1895 to give atmosphere and illumination
on the darkest nights, the parts hauled in
by ox carts. Guaranteed by the Fort Wayne Electric Company
to make a pocket watch readable at 1500 feet,
or they'd haul them off again. What an age! Telegraphs,
telephones and artificial moonlight! The Titan Prometheus
carrying fire to heaven, rivaling the moon.
Making the sun would come later.

The lamplighter went up the pole daily
to change the carbon filaments.
Now the lamps last three years, an electric eye
wakes them up to work their night shift.
Seventeen are still standing.

Number eighteen was saved from destruction
by picketing protestors on a building site,
but the next day the contractor's crane
accidentally knocked it down.

I went back later to test the old guarantee
with my wrist watch, pocket models
having dropped into the oubliette of time
along with the ox carts. I could see it was 11 o'clock,
late in the Twentieth Century, an age cluttered with wonders.

Feeding the Power Grid

As we drove through the Battle River valley
he gave us a social history of the farms
on the east side of the road: who had died
childless; whose children moved to town
and sold the land to strangers; who is banned
from owning any cattle after the winter
twenty of them stood starving inside
a fancy electrified fence. Once in a while
the stories are racy: "That guy married a big woman
with hair on her face who could whip
a grizzly bear with a switch." He doesn't look once
to the west, where great mounds of fresh clay
have been tossed up by the drag lines. The strip mine
will pursue the coal a hundred meters down
to feed the power grids of Western Canada.
This was the farm where he and my wife grew up,
the place where their mother's ashes were scattered.
"Dust to dust," "the common clay"—fine phrases,
but the mine goes deeper than gossip or Genesis:
there was no oral history in the Cretaceous.
His past burns like filaments in a light bulb.

East Coulee

I know the evolution of company towns,
having grown up in one
with the routine of whistles
and the bondage of the company store.
East Coulee was bedroom to the Atlas Mine.
The coal screening plant stands near the hillside
with the long chute of the tipple
joining it to the mine opening
Now the revenue is from the tape-guided tours.
Atlas doesn't shoulder much of the burden any more.

A man in East Coulee makes grey birdhouses
duplicating the plant, with a thick perch
as the tipple.
              I hate to think of bluebirds
setting up house in a dark image of a mine.
The town has shrunk to 150 people,
a decline of 95%.
Mostly they live in little shingled houses
built by the company.
One house has a back yard planted thick
with a dozen kinds of lilies
and some shafts of delphiniums.
The yard is like a terrace with a drop
of six feet to the neighbor's yard.
There are beams and wedges
to slow an inevitable slide.
Nebuchadnezzar would be proud
of such a hanging garden.

The one industry that thrives
is the Prehistoric Animal Simulation Team,

which makes replicas of dinosaurs
for parks and museums.
The economy has moved
from coal to man-made reptiles.
Before the last inhabitants go,
I wish the town a tiny Eohippus,
the four-toed ancestral horse,
to chase out of the lily beds.

Armageddon at Endiang, Alberta

Outside Stettler the Chamber of Commerce sign says,
"Future Home of a World-Class Grain Handling Facility."
Endiang down the road was once declared
the most likely spot for Russian and US missiles
to meet each other if the Russians fired first,
but no Chamber of Commerce
would put up a sign saying, "Future Home
of World War III." Endiang is famous enough
for its duck and goose hunting, and the deer,
which can strip a wheat field almost as fast
as a honking crowd of Canada geese.
Farmers buy hunting blinds shaped
like the big rolls of hay in the meadows.
Bing Crosby used to come to Endiang,
for the duck season, but hardly anyone
remembers him, his image fading like Krushchev's.
The hotel has three rooms, over the tavern:
the Deer Room with mural wallpaper
showing a dark forest and suspicious deer
poised among the trees, the Duck Room
with a procession of mallards beak to tail
on a wallpaper frieze around the room,
and the Bridal Suite, a room unconsummated
by honeymooners. Roy Maguire never
sleeps in the Deer Room, the dim forest
gives him nightmares. He likes the Duck Room,
and tonight he lies drunk on the squeaking bed
with his boots on, aiming his 20 gauge at the frieze.
He has no shell in the chamber, just stretches out
taking aim, taking aim: click, click, click.
He'll lie snoring all night, his arms wrapped
around the walnut stock of the shotgun.

Van Horne

"Once I built a railroad, I made it run, I made it race against time.
Once I built a railroad, now it's done. Brother, can you spare a dime?"
— E. Y. Harburg

You could call him a Renaissance man if you tailored the Renaissance to him. Big and bulgy he called himself, with an office full of armless chairs to ease his sitting and standing. William Van Horne, that is, Sir William Van Horne, a native of Iowa, who knelt for the accolade, dubbed a knight for building the railroad across Canada. A man who smoked cigars and played poker, which he said was not a game but an education; a sensitive man who bought Rembrandts and Cezannes and liked to handle Japanese porcelains in his enormous hands. An amateur paleontologist who learned geology as a boy by copying out Hitchcock's ELEMENTS word for word, picture for picture. Once he saw a fossil in a city pavement and came with a chisel to chip it out. A man who retired by going to Cuba, where the cigars came from, and building a railway across the country. Who was limited to three cigars a day by his doctor and had them made a foot long, knowing that an engineer must spout smoke and ashes like a steam engine. Who never had to say, "Brother, can you spare a dime?" Who painted brilliant pictures and sometimes signed them with famous names, laughing at those who were taken in. Whose picture in the Art Gallery of Ontario holds its modest space on the wall with honor: "The Sand Pit," beautifully composed and showing an engineer's eye for raw materials, because you never know when you might want to build a railway.

Bears

I have thoughts about bears to lick into shape.
I am happy to contemplate them
but wouldn't want to meet a grizzly—
ursus horribilis horribilis—on a mountain path.
My great-grandfather, Will Bryson,
toured the South with wrestling bears,
and I notice in the old photograph
that he has the she-bear and her cub in muzzles.
Monkeys and apes look more like us,
but with a touch of parody, while a bear
can walk upright but has fur and dog-like snout.

At the *Jardin des Plantes*, my son and I
saw a display of bears: the Paleolithic Bear in Art,
and accounts of the bear in chivalric romances—
Valentine and Ourson were brothers,
one raised as a knight, the other as a bear,
and the knightly brother tamed the ursine one,
a very French fable. French too were the exhibits
on The Bear in Myth and Symbol, and The Bear
in Popular Custom. Nothing about bear-baiting,
the old Anglo-Saxon pastime. The bear for children
had its own section: mechanical bears and teddies,
and the famous bears of literature:
Rupert, Paddington from darkest Peru,
Mischka, Prosper, Baloo and Winnie l'ourson.
The porridge-eating nuclear family
had no names, just their generational tags.
I thought of the Hollywood bear, Orson Welles,
who turned into his orotund given name.
These were bears seen through the grid
of French culture, curated into tameness.

But walking out, we strolled through the park
and saw a dramatic statue of a man
being eaten by a bear. Not long ago
an English wildlife painter was killed by a grizzly.
The rangers found it gnawing on his shoulder.
There was that evolutionary social-climber,
the black bear in Banff who walked up
to the Douglas Fir Chalets and learned to open
the automatic doors. He'd move back and forth,
commanding the door to open, then letting it shut.
After a while he climbed into a pick-up truck
and was sitting in the driver's seat drinking a carton
of chocolate milk when the rangers shot him.
A terrible error: if he had put on a tractor cap
and popped a country music tape
in the cassette player, he'd have overtaken
the human race at its lower reaches.

Spanghew

Slang, chiefly Brit.: to toss a frog violently into the air from the end of a stick.

Martin Heidegger said we're all thrown
into the world—but not as violently as that—
and a Greek poet said "the boys throw stones
at the frogs in sport, but the frogs die in earnest."
In my childhood the five-and-dime sold
turtles with painted shells and Easter chicks
dyed blue or green or pink. My sister had two chicks,
and they couldn't survive her earnest love.
I remember a turtle of my own, the shell painted
bright blue, with my hometown lettered in red.
What a fictional killer I was in the pictures
from one of my birthdays, with a cowboy hat
and shiny cap gun. The caps came in long red strips
with buttons of gunpowder to slaughter the peace
of the neighborhood. I can smell the smoke. The turtle
was last seen struggling to climb out of its bowl.

Reconnaisance Flight

1.
I thought it was a paramedic helicopter,
but it kept circling, then I knew there were two,
not quite in synch, and they were landing in the park
behind our house. What was it, a SWAT team
for the quarrelsome neighbors, a drug raid?

The pilots set their craft down facing each other,
then got out, walked to the midpoint and shook hands.

Were they going to exchange microfilm for money,
or switch a spy from one agency to another?

One smoked cigarettes, the other opened his Thermos.
They had an amiable tête-à-tête
and then took off, the hinged blades beating,
too loud as always, too loud, circling
all afternoon. The small propellor on the tail
compensates for the torque on the blades.

2.
Two days earlier we had gone to the ravine near our house
to see if the saskatoon berries at the edge of the woods
were ripe yet. A nervous man asked us about the ravine,
the berries, the wild flowers. We pointed out the wild roses
at the border of the thicket, the saskatoon bushes behind them,
and a little deeper, the white anemones with their five petals.
And where did the woods lead to, he asked.
I told him about the trails down the slope, the footbridge
over the creek. I warned him about wasp stings.
He thanked us. We'd see him again in the paper.

3.
The fat robin in my garden hops about gathering straw
and bits of twig in its beak. What I don't understand,
no matter how closely I watch, is how it adds each piece
to the ones it already has without dropping any.
It pauses to listen to the cautionary cries of its mate.

4.
He'd gone missing after a visit to the doctor.
The day after the search was called off,
his wife found the body under the footbridge,
which had been used as the control post
for the searchers with their dogs, radios,
and infrared scanners.
It was like a prank by the dead man,
playing hide-and-seek and hiding at home base.
And like a folktale figure, I guided him to death,
with instructions coded as a nature lecture.

The anemone got its name from the Greeks—
anemos, the wind. The flowers open, they thought,
with the spring breezes. The wood anemone shines
like a white star in the shade where it grows.

Fires

Motel Parking Lot

A few minutes after I called the switchboard
and complained about the noisy band in the bar,
the switchboard called me. The music had stopped.
I expected an apology, but the operator said,
"Don't go back to sleep right away,
we think the motel may be on fire."
Smoke with a chemical smell
starting coming out of the registers.
My wife and I spent the next hour
in a cold car, with two little girls
wearing coats over their nightgowns.

The next morning in the coffee shop
a man with a Tasmanian Devil t-shirt
was telling and retelling his story:
he heard the old man screaming
in his burning chair, how the door
just popped open when he kicked it.
I could hear self-astonishment
as well as pride in his voice,
and I was pleased every time
the waitress refilled his coffee cup.
We like the unlikely heroes best.
"The old fellow's going to make it.
I'm glad I went looking for the ice machine,"
he told everyone. "That door just popped open."

A Sidewalk

Cate went to Philadelphia one night
and missed Jamie's party. The next morning
she went by the house on a walk and found
heaps of wet ashes. She thought,
Jamie must have gotten out,
maybe the dog was killed,
but she must have gotten out.
Then footsteps behind her, a neighbor
with a voice full of grief.

The young woman looking at the ashes
was a child shivering in the back seat of a car.
Now she stood desolate,
in a story without a warning phone call,
without a rescuer who just happened by.
Grief was the measure of her love,
a measure no one wants taken, the steel tape
that should stay coiled tightly in its case.

The Cartoonist

The director walked gently across the thick carpet
and held out his hand. "Dr. Schiff, I'm so sorry
that your father has passed away," he murmured.
During the arrangements, talk about careers
led the director to confess: "I always wanted to be
a cartoonist, but what could I do,
this is the family business." He became wistful,
said he wanted nothing more
than to sit all day at a drafting board
with a set of sharpened pencils. "My God,
some of the things that happen around here
practically draw themselves. In fact,
I've got a few in my desk here." Another bereaved
came into the room without knocking.
"Pardon me for a moment." The director walked
delicately across the carpet: "Dr. Stone, I'm so sorry
that your mother has passed away." This time
the soft words floated over his head,
Gothic type in a black-bordered balloon.

The Gargoyle

All through another long winter afternoon
her teacher, Dr. Standish, evades his topic,
the history of the subjunctive mood,
by talking about sex: he loves to describe
the Roman garden-statues of Priapus,
whose penis was so long he was depicted
hoisting it over his shoulder. Dr. Standish
likes to mime that with an imaginary heave.
Drifting into daydream as he snickers on,
she recalls her wheezing and dirty neighbor
hiking a leaky old garden hose
over his shoulder as he carried it to the rubbish pile.

Dust of History

The young man in the Pancho Villa Bar
on Swallow Street, Piccadilly Circus,
bragged he was Darth Vader's son.
"Oh, do you have a lung disease too?"
"No, no, my dad was the actor,
but they dubbed the voice of James Earl Jones.
Now Dad plays the Green Crossing Knight
in the safety ads." "Ah, I always knew
they were the same: who's ever seen
them together, Lord Death and Sir Caution?"

A waitress in a sombrero took a shot glass
from one of the cartridge belts crossing her chest
and drew a bottle of tequila from her right holster.
She put one foot up on a chair, slapping her thigh
and counting till Darth Vader's son
choked down his slug of cactus juice.

Poor Pancho Villa was a teetotaler,
but Hollywood wrote that out of the scripts.
Outside the bar, his statue sits
life-sized on a bronze horse,
in full gallop like a B-movie still.
Villa rode from history into myth into nowhere:
the terror of Northern Mexico, and now
someone goes over him daily with a feather-duster.

¡Salúd, Hombre!

Value Village

My daughter Cate searched hundreds of racks for retro clothes in this emporium of forks with bent prongs and eight-track stereos with one speaker. A young friend found a Hermès scarf here for $1.50: a grandma's green silk printed with belts and buckles from the 1970s, mistaken for rayon by the survivors. Hermes, god of commerce, god of thieves, presides in this place but bestows his blessings grudgingly. I watched two old men, three canes between them, a riddle to baffle the Sphinx, intent on something caught in a jumble of chairs and tables in the back of the store. The man with two canes leaned on one and was fishing in the maze of furniture with the other. His friend was scoffing: "You'll never get it around that runner, then there's the coffee table jammed into the easy chair, you might as well quit." But the man finally slid a penny out, and stooping took it between fingers knobbed with arthritis. "You know," said his friend, "it's the person who spots the penny who gets the luck, not the one who picks it up." I left them to argue the metaphysics of destiny. Down the next aisle I had to dodge the hooker pushing the wheelchair of a man in cowboy clothes whose body seemed frozen in a spasm. I could hear the cracked voices of the old men rising: Luck with her gilded wings must have hovered in the air between them, unwilling to go with either, knowing that in the Kingdom of As-Is she has doubtful jurisdiction.

The Shot Tower

I want to think of poems as if made in a shot tower,
a tall building where molten lead poured through a sieve
drops a long way, with surface tension forming
perfect spheres, annealed by the plunge
into the cold water tank at the bottom.

Instead I confront a bored detective
digging a misshapen bullet out of a wall
after it missed the target. A leaden clot
dropped into a plastic bag but marked
by human choice. Pure gravity writes no poetry.

Between Heaven and Hell

As I walk into the medical arts centre,
the security guard looks up from her desk:
"Purgatory: a place for those who are too bad
to go to heaven, and too good to go to hell."
Not a message from the fates, I think.
I can see her pencil hovering
over a crossword puzzle. Purgatory in my case
is an elevator ride to the fifth floor,
where Tyra massages a sub-occipital muscle
the size of a fingernail. In spasm, a coal from hell.
Tyra is on the side of the angels,
I know that: she has angel posters
and an angelic candle whose head
has melted onto its neck and wings.
Tyra reads my palm as she massages my fingers,
and tells me my life line is very long.
"My life line is all messed up," she says.
She wants to talk quantum physics: "Dr. Hawking
disappointed me, I knew all that stuff already."
She assures me that time is unreal.
"What about your appointments," I ask,
you need time to keep track of them."
"I always know when a client won't show
and I never come for those." She's here, I'm here,
QED I won't argue with her logic,
not with my head and neck melting into blissful wax.
She gives me a coupon, "Good for One Free Hug
from Any Human Being." On my way out,
I decide against offering it to the security guard.

Wanting as a Tendency to Act

"That Smith went to the store because he believed he was out of bread is accepted as an explanation only on the assumption that Smith wanted bread."

⇢ *Encyclopedia of Philosophy*

Hands come and go in the fridge in the Philosophy Lounge. At 11:45 AM on March 11, 1999 the eye discovers on the bottom shelf, a half-empty jug of Cranapple Juice, abandoned months ago. On the second shelf, an opened package of salted butter and one box (250 ml) of mixed tropical fruit juices (no less than 10% real juice—pineapple, papaya, passion fruit), vitamin C added. Beside the juice box, a clear plastic bag with two dozen little cream-coloured cylinders of non-dairy creamer. On the top shelf, three lunches in paper bags bearing initials in felt-tip marker, and three glass jars of human milk.

The nose discovers that the fridge needs cleaning, but no one is responsible for doing so. <I helped the old man out of pity> is not the same as <I helped the old man out of mud> but there is a connection. If we understood, someone would clean the fridge.

The eye in time lapse mode observes a montage of hands flickering in and out of the fridge, seeking or leaving the necessities of life. By 5:30 the big ruby of Cranapple Juice reposes alone behind the white door. On the other side of the door, the Philosophers' Colloquium is contending over coffee about reasons and causes: <under conditions such that> and <consequently>. Someone claims that a want and an intention must be connected by a belief. In the last row the female graduate student rocks her baby while the male graduate student tests the temperature of its bottle by shaking a few drops on his wrist.

The author studied philosophy with Wittgenstein at Cambridge. The tutorials were held in a pub called The Flying Pig, where a signboard behind the bar always read:

>Realist Cheap Night
>A pint for the price of a pint
>Oink!

The Seven Deadlies Updated: A Pageant
(Anger, Pride, Covetousness, Gluttony, Envy, Lust, Sloth)

Road Rage
He invoked the divine right of SUVs
to run a Hyundai into the ditch
Losing control he hit a light standard
It was engineered to snap neatly
as his neck did between C5 and C6

Stanley Cup-Size
He found her in the personals
where she flaunted being
"the ex-girlfriend of an Oiler"

He likes to tell people
about the ex-boyfriend's
scoring statistics

As for his own
he smirks a little
and talks about hat tricks

Inside Trader
His hedge fund sold stocks short
with the aid of a little data
from employees of the companies

Unable to pick up anything now
at plea-bargain basement prices
he finds he sold his future short

Anorexic
When she got home from the clinic
and her mother asked her

was she going to turn over a new leaf
she had visions of a sea of tossed salad:
lettuce shards floating in an oil-slick of Canola

Rasta Wannabe
He's had his blond hair dreaded
with the $400 perm
He listens to reggae in class
on his iPod and at lunch hour
hangs out near the black guys
to troll for slang   After school
he drives his Beamer home
with the burglar alarm code
running through his mind
like a guilty secret

Groupie
"I took a rhinestone off my cocktail dress
and told him I'd like to insert it in his navel
with my tongue   That did it, and we slipped away

I remembered to turn the lock but who expected
the goddam bathroom to have two doors?"

Channel Surfer
Deep in the thousand-channel universe
he was watching *The Talking-Animal Comedy Network*
at the moment when the war started
The single-channel universe went out of service
just as Mr. Ed was making
a comment on human folly
in that slow ironic drawl

My Winter Sport

I thought I could never be Canadian unless I had a winter sport.

I tried snowshoeing but the shoes look like tennis rackets
and why play a game where love means zero?

Downhill skiing was out after all those cartoons
reducible to parallel lines approaching a circle:
I want to hug trees but not that hard.

My friend Fred put me off cross country skiing.
He believes fiberglass skis are ersatz
and carries three waxes so that he can redo the wood
as the quality of the snow changes during the day.
I thought of Julian Bream's joke: play the lute
for twenty years and you'll have spent ten years tuning it.

I stood on knife blades at a frozen pond just once,
figuring that if I lowered myself gently to the ice
I could say that I've never fallen while skating.
As for curling, the sound of the rock reminds me of bowling:
I wait and wait for the crash of a strike that never comes.

One day my son forgot his hockey stick.
I was taking it to him when I met our neighbor
who never speaks to anyone: he looked at me
and said, "Do you really play, or is that just for show?"

I recalled the prophecy made to Odysseus,
that he would live in peace in his land
after he carried an oar into a desert
so far that someone would ask him,

"Stranger, what is that great winnowing fan on your shoulder?"
Then he could plant the oar in the sand and go home.

Next winter I'll walk into the Sonora desert with a hockey stick
until I find someone to ask me, "Stranger,
what's that slender oar you have on your shoulder?"
And that will be my Canadian winter sport: hiking in Arizona.

The Holy Family

1.
It was like Henry James novel
for the 1970s: the Belgravia house,
the drawing room with dark carved paneling
and an Old Master painting
of the Holy Family. A museum
had offered a half million for the panels,
though opinion was divided
about the provenance: some said
16th century Flemish, others
swore Grinling Gibbons,
an absurd disharmony of experts.

I asked my wife about the Old Master.
"Look closer," she said: Mary and Joseph
had the faces of our hosts, the shepherds
and shepherdess were their three children.

I squirmed on the sofa, remembering
Sunday school, the hard text I learned by heart
from Galatians: *God is not mocked*,
harder maybe than *the wages of sin is death*.
Rely on St. Paul to put it bluntly.

2.
The big surprise had been the greeting
at the door by the husband, who was living
with his daughter's best friend, ex-best
friend now. He pretended to be the happy
paterfamilias. His wife and children ignored him.
The mistress must have been eating alone
in her expensive flat across town.

The tax man on this case was probably
working late at his desk, eating take-away food.

3.
(The Inland Revenue settled the family affairs
after a series of deaths and divorces
and the house became an embassy,
bought by an ex-colony in the Pacific,
or some successor state of a former country.
The carvings must still be *in situ*,
but I don't know who got the paintings.)

4.
We had a play to go to, *Noises Off*,
which *The Times* had called
the greatest farce of all time—
amorous intrigues and countless
botched entrances and exits.
So we made our goodbyes
and went out to hail a taxi,
happy to see the black car
coming up the street.
We didn't mind the driver's
wild dash to the theatre.

D'Arcy Wentworth Thompson

1.
My mother worked for the Ideal Laundry
between dropping out of school and having me.
She always feared those instruments of order,
the wringer, the mangle, the trouser-press.
I think of her when I read D'Arcy Thompson,
who had his choice of three professorships at 23:
Classics, Mathematics or Zoology. He could
construe garbled Greek texts and interpret
all the scholia, and he described the growth
of the nautilus shell with logarithmic spirals.
His *Growth and Form* explains why a moth
flies to the lamp in a decaying orbit rather than
a straight line: it has compound eyes and can see
anywhere but straight ahead, so it steers
in a contracting spiral, though it's as thirsty
for the bulb as St. Lawrence was for the gridiron.
Professor Thompson's neat equations
precisely render the moth's approximations.

2.
On Professor Thompson's zoology final,
there was always a skeleton he'd assembled
from half a dozen different animals. The question
said, "What is this?" The proper answer was, "I don't know."
A desperate student would turn the bones over,
find a small printed placard that read, "Horse,"
and happily answer the question, "horse,"
never suspecting that ignorance could be knowledge.

3.
Once a boy on top of a tram said: "Are ye Professor Thompson?"
"Aye, lad, I am." "Well, do ye ken a lot?" "Aye, lad,
I ken a lot." "But I ken somethin ye dunna ken."
"And what might that be, lad?" The boy fingered
his shirt placket and tugged it toward the Professor.
"I ken my mother does your laundry, and this is *your* shirt!"

Professor Thompson's shirt turns up everywhere,
delivering us from accuracy and the jaws of the mangle.
I've worn it once or twice: my mother stole it
from a drawstring bag at the Ideal Laundry.

for Angus Ross

Honeysuckle

Or better:
honey
suckle
What could be light enough
to be suckled by the orange flowers
of the vine reaching over
the fence from the neighbor's
in a patient tropism of touch?
Bees of course
though even a bumblebee
might be too awkward
for the slender funnel

The other day at dusk
glancing out the big window
I thought I saw a dragonfly
hovering near the blossoms
and then corrected myself
as the bird delicately probed
a flower on the vine

I called out to our guests
and the painter
who hasn't seen everything
but has seen everything he sees
saw something for the first time:
a hummingbird
now sitting in profile
on one of the tendrils

the only bird whose weight
the branch could bear
could bear
without bending

Tiger's Eye

Country-bred, you like country metaphors,
and when I asked you to describe the exact colour
of your yellow-brown eyes, you said: "They're the colour
of spring run-off." And so they are: now I look
for your bright glance in the rivulets of March.
I gave you a strand of tiger's-eye beads, the same brown,
chatoyant stones that shine like the eyes of a cat
because the quartz is filled with fibers of iron oxide.
As you laugh, shrug your shoulders, turn your head, light
swirls through the quartz, through the pigments of your eyes,
every sparkle of light a motion of spring.

Austin City Limits

1. *The Bible in the Harry Ransom Center*
The letters imitate *textura*, a Gothic script
with equal verticals and a little foot, a black point,
for each bold character. He made inks like a chemist:
the black was a cooked copper-lead oxide,
not carbon, so it has never browned on the page.
The type faces were cast in molds of fine sand
and inked by a ball stuffed with horsehair.
Every leaf has been digitized now,
but the book still lies open in a glass case,
with its thick black tessellations on the white paper.

Austin is full of scholars, but does any
excel the friendly cab driver who told me,
"I just have to go down to the Ransom Center
and look at that Gutenberg Bible once a year."

2. *Roy's Taxis*
    I remember the taxi driver in Shoreham-by-Sea who wore a Greek fisherman's hat and sat very upright in his Lada: he had served in the Irish guards. And I couldn't forget the Karaoke cab in San Francisco, the driver inviting me to sing Elvis songs with the Jordanaires, but this was my first lactating cab driver, *Laurel* it says on the receipt, who picked me up at the airport in Austin and told me she was very drowsy, having stopped at her house to feed the baby. She kept trying to speed up in the traffic to cool off the engine and told me she was 39 and thought she'd never have a baby but the test came positive on Valentine's Day. I think Laurel if you had played a Karaoke tape with steel guitars I would have improvised a country song on the spot but right then I was remembering the little

Madonna by a minor Flemish master that I saw at the Fitzwilliam Museum in Cambridge, the baby absolutely drowsy with milk on his lips and the young mother far from 39 but full of grace or bliss at this unexpected turn in her life.

Austin Odyssey

If I sit in the dark on the patio
of the bed-and-breakfast
feasting with three empty chairs
drinking Pecan St. Beer against the heat
and eating a barbecue sandwich
that passes for roasted ox
—if I sit alone in the dark
with Whiskers the cat
as my apathetic only companion
Then I find my mind singing
with dislocated motifs from the Odyssey—

Because three times tonight
a muttering emeritus has walked by
a nonagenarian version of Nestor

Because this afternoon I sailed
along Guadalupe Street
at the University campus
past the slackers caught in lotus dreams
wearing their dirty army fatigues
flashing their home-made tattoos
their pierced tongues and nostrils

Because early this morning
I passed a beautiful woman
in a short night gown
who was walking her mastiff
And when I told my Penelope

in an e-mail, she typed back
"Odysseus you'd better steer clear
of that young Circe"

I have no sign from Athena
though I spent all day
in the Humanities Research Center
I think she has abandoned the emeritus
who just walked by again
escorted by his faithful wife

On the way back tonight I passed
frat houses where party-goers caroused
like drunken suitors
There's a movie called *Sirens*
showing in the Union Theatre
It's full of breasts
jiggling in the Australian Outback

If I feel like a lost mariner
in the middle of this parched city
it's because I can imagine
the presence of the limestone layer
under the thin topsoil
—the gardener's curse
laid down 350 million years ago
when the sea covered Texas
It's because I feel I've been away
almost that long

An ash tree as high as the roof
brushes our bedroom window at home
When I finish my beer and sandwich
I can go inside and place a call to that room
a thought that turns the sultry night intimate
so that I take a deep breath on this patio
suddenly tasting the wine-dark air

Indian Lodge

1.
In the courtyard
the madrone tree
(a California native
but growing nicely here)
sheds pink bark in streamers
the way other trees shed leaves

The madrone stands
an exiled queen
in tattered robes
or a lingerie model
keeping Victoria's secret

2.
This morning I drove
to the McDonald Observatory
In the cool dome
the telescope rests
so lightly balanced
a flashlight battery
has the power to move it

Ruby pulses from its mirror
bouncing off a reflector
in the Sea of Tranquillity
are a stake to mark
the drift of the continent
under our feet

Birds entered the dome
through the slot
twittered all through the guide's lecture

3.
At Indian Lodge
swallows have built nests
high on the white stacked walls
I love their swoop to the nest
the slight twist to enter it
as if the ghost
of a remorseful pickpocket
were slipping a wallet
back where it came from

The madrone is a slender woman
standing in gauzy garments
in the moonlight
Negligée I murmur
Deshabillée I whisper
but she speaks only Spanish

Curled up in bed tonight
I lie very still
and try to sense the drift
of the continent

Covered with White Cloth, the Grail Enters the Chapel Perilous

Let me call him Professor Inkling,
though he personified
the legend of absentmindedness,
unable to find anything in his office,
never able to keep an appointment.
Once or twice a year one of his articles
on an esoteric subject—
like Arthurian motifs in the poetry of Charles Williams—
would appear in an obscure journal.
He was a legend for never bathing,
but someone who'd been to his apartment
provided an explanation:
the bathtub was full of books.

But he considered himself blessed
because one Christmas Eve
walking from the station
he saw a phone box illuminated in the fog
and felt there was a reason to enter it,
although he had no one to call.
A newborn baby lay sleeping on the floor.
He carried it to the lost-and-found
in the police station. It might have died,
so he carries that event like a chalice,
the night that an inner nudge
made him remember something he'd never known.

The Feast of St. Valentine's

Edmonton/Stettler/Edmonton

Imagine—
spending Valentine's Day
fetching a side of beef from the country:
that's what our son called out as we drove away.
Romance is where you find it, I thought.
While the butcher's boy fetched the hand truck
full of rock-hard packages from the freezer,
I looked over the paper on the wall,
the Licence to Operate an Abattoir.
When I first saw *abattoir* in a book
I thought it was the most beautiful word
in the world. Romance is how you hear it.
Once I was sure that venison
must be the best meat in the world,
just from the sound of it. It meant
hunting in Sherwood Forest with Maid Marian
and the feasting and music afterward.
You and I can make a feast with hamburger.
Romance is how you taste it.
We had lunch with your relatives
in the White Goose Restaurant,
where Valentine's meant paper hearts on the walls,
a rose on each table. Your brother Ivan,
who raised that frozen critter,
kidded me, saying we men had better have oysters
if it's Valentine's day. I did, and all the way
to the city I thought of roses:
the antique shop called The White Rose
made me remember the old brands,
Five Roses Flour and Four Roses Whisky,

the little miracles of yeast.
Romance is where you see it.
Just before the city, we drove by
The Lucky Horseshoe Ranch,
a most auspicious name,
and my heart raced in a delirium
brought on by the oysters,
or Cupid nudging me in the ribs with an arrow.
Romance is how you feel it.

Frieze of Life

"Birth and Life at the Fin de Siecle—
Symbolist Europe: Lost Paradise"

My daughter found her favorite painting
pasted on fences and walls all over Montréal—
Klimt's "Hope I," the naked pregnant woman
in profile with her head turned to the viewer.
Faces and a skull scowl in the upper margin.
I had Cate stand outside the Musée des Beaux Arts
by that poster and took her picture.
In it she looks up, her eyes closed in the sunlight.
The museum shop had the ultimate kitsch souvenir,
an inflatable model of Munch's "The Scream,"
part of his *Frieze of Life* series, Berlin,
1902. It would be a pleasure to buy
the little inflatable grotesque
and let it deflate with an ignoble noise,
the distorted face distorting further.
A candidate for picture of the century?
Or do we go with the shyness under threat
of Klimt's pregnant redhead, painted the year
after Munch's howling cartoon? My favorite Klimt
is "Schubert at the Piano." The candles
have turned the women's dresses to light
as they stand listening in the fragile spell of art.
Schubert sits in a band of shadow in the picture.
Painted two years before the new century, it failed
to outlive it: *1945 Verbrannt*, the reproduction says.

My photograph has no threatening margins:
my own child is my best symbol of hope.

Leonid Shower

Like a broom, the earth
sweeps through the comet's litter,
if we can imagine the broom
setting the dust on fire:
fading streaks of ionized gas
all coming from the same point
in the sky—the radiant—
as one orbit intersects another.

In 1833 all of America
thought the world was ending
and filled the churches to pray.
The Cherokee called it
"the night the stars fell."
A harmless apocalypse,
not a call to judgment.

On the last day of his life,
Michael Lazar rose early
to watch the stars falling.
A friend wrote later,
"It was almost as if
messengers from another world
had come to light his way."
That "almost as if"
measures the distance from our day
to the first night the stars fell.

Michael worked on the fractal compression
of video images: like an oak tree
endlessly branching, packed into an acorn.

He held his son's blanket to his face
as his wife drove to the hospital.
She calmed the frightened child by singing,
"the wheels on the bus go round and round."

We sing, we pray, we watch the sky,
and sometimes we are anointed with fire.

Ada Sweet

Beaumont, Texas
Ada thought she'd try the care of the sick,
a way to take her mind off her husband's death.
When she came driving up, I didn't think I could bear it:
the old purple Buick was out of a racist joke.
She was covered with costume jewelry
and a tooth flashed gold in her smile.
My mother needed a helper, and liked rhinestones herself.
The crisis was not the salary but the moment
I asked her to call me Bert, putting it as fair play:
"If you're Ada, then I have to be Bert." She frowned a long time,
then finally said, "Okay, Mister Bert," not understanding
my liberal humiliation. A sharecropper's daughter,
she had escaped into thirty-five years of cooking
at a Ramada Inn, and married a part-time Baptist preacher.

2.
Standing in for a son who lived in another country,
Ada performed four of the Seven Works
of Corporal Mercy daily for my mother.
Tending the Sick required three of the others:
Feeding the Hungry
by coaxing food into a mouth raw
with the sores of the thrush infection
induced by chemotherapy;
Giving Drink
to the thirsty by holding a glass with a straw
or offering cracked ice wrapped in a cloth
when swallowing was too painful;
Clothing the Naked

by guiding feet into hose, hose into shoes,
legs into skirt, arms into sleeves. All this
gently, patiently.

When I tried to praise her
she would give the credit to Jesus,
and I wouldn't dare to disagree,
after being reduced to the elevation of "Mister Bert."

3.
The Seventh Work of Corporal Mercy
is the Burial of the Dead, which came to me. Afterward,
Ada said, "I couldn't do this kind of job again,
you come to like the person too much."

I thought when I met her that she
had never heard of Martin Luther King, but finally
I was sure she never heard of President Lincoln:
leaving, she put her bags down
before my wife and stood patiently
on feet spread flat from those years
in the kitchen of the Ramada Inn. "Ada,
what are you waiting for?"
"I thought you'd want to check my bags
to be sure I haven't taken anything."
My wife broke into tears,
and Ada said, "Honey, I didn't mean to make you cry."
The stern Fathers of the Church overlooked
tears as a corporal work of mercy.

Coffeewood Court

Driveway

The pepper tree hanging over the driveway
bears green, white, pink and red peppercorns.
Getting out of the car we crunch fallen berries,
raising a mild scent of pepper. The canopy of slender leaves
filters the California sun. The sign on the garage door reads:

**ATTENTION
CHIEN BIZARRE**

Jasper, the Australian sheep dog, has a docked tail,
but he wags his whole body in greeting. He's all right, mate.

Patio

Lesley brings the gin and tonic, a drink of essences:
blue-green juniper berries and quinine bark,
elemental flavors refined into clarity.
Tony has gathered chanterelles. Scented with earth,
they rest on newspaper on the kitchen counter,
destined for tomorrow's omelet. We sit on the patio,
Jasper watching us with his toy shark between his teeth.
He must regret that the big grassy yard has no flock
for him to tend. His instincts are all for care and vigilance.

Across San José the Rosicrucian Museum
has a hall of Egyptian bric-a-brac and a planetarium.
We could go there and learn about planetary deities
and the meaning of symbols like the eye in the pyramid.

But I can see that unblinking pyramid on the US bills
in my wallet, and the planets find their way without shepherds.
If my ears ring, it's the effect of the quinine
rather than the music of the spheres.
This is enough: the benign chanterelles
in a golden heap on yesterday's toxic headlines,
and the toy shark safe in the sheepdog's mouth.

for Tony and Lesley Mason

Acknowledgements

Many of these poems first appeared in magazines: *The Antigonish Review, Ariel, Borderlands: A Texas Review, Canadian Literature, Concho River Review, Event, The Fiddlehead, Grain, JCT: An International Curriculum Quarterly, Jones Av., Lines Review, The Malahat Review, Mattoid, New Quarterly, Nimrod, The Olive, Other Poetry, Other Voices, Quadrant, Queen's Quarterly, Southern Review, Tandem, Texas Observer, TickleAce, The Times Literary Supplement, The Windhover, University of Windsor Review, Zygote.*

Others were anthologized:

"Frieze of Life." *Vintage 98*, Vancouver: Ronsdale Press, 1999.
"Feeding the Power Grid" and "Hampstead Elegies," *Threshold: An Anthology of Contemporary Writing from Alberta*. Edmonton: University of Alberta Press, 1999.
"Austin Odyssey," *New Texas 2000*. Belton: Center for Texas Studies, 2001.
"Dove Cottage," "The Bible in the Harry Ransom Center," "My Ménage à Trois," and "Glen Iris Tram," *Winnowings*. Geelong, Australia: Deakin University, 2003.
"The Shot Tower." *The Harbrace Anthology of English Literature*. Toronto: 2006.

"A Ghost in Waterloo Station" was the runner-up in the 2001 *Times Literary Supplement* / Blackwell's Poetry Competition.

I wrote "The Apprentice Pillar, Rosslyn Chapel," during a fellowship at the International Writer's Residence Centre at Hawthornden Castle, which is operated through the benevolence of Drew Heinz. I am indebted to Moira Shearer, who drove me to Rosslyn.

Some of the poems were written with the assistance of a Senior Arts Grant from the Alberta Foundation for the Arts.

I must thank a number of people who read these poems with a critical and sympathetic eye: Olga Costopoulos, Meli Costopoulos, Shawna Lemay, Don Domanski, John Reibetanz, Robert Burlingame, Lee Elliott, Iman Mersal, Kimmy Beach, Michael Penny, Michael McCarthy, and Ian Gough. The poems owe much to the hospitality of Angus and Diana Ross, Heather Agboola, Leslie Stretch, Morgan Kenney, Kurt Wagar, and Deborah Goodall.

Gratitude is due to the editors and staff of Brindle & Glass: Ruth Linka, Lee Shedden, Lisa Martin-DeMoor, and Diane Shaw, for their care in producing this book.

BERT ALMON is the author of eight previous collections of poetry, including *Earth Prime* which won the 1995 Writer's Guild of Alberta Award for Poetry. He has been a finalist for the *Times Literary Supplement* / Blackwell's Poetry Competition, and in 1993 was a Poetry Fellow at Hawthornden Castle, Scotland. He has taught modern literature and creative writing at the University of Alberta since 1968 and at least thirty of his former students have gone on to publish their own collections of poetry (more than fifty books).